Peaceful Protests:

VOICES FOR PEACE

Jane Addams, Muhammad Ali,
John Lennon, Leymah Gbowee

Wayne L. Wilson

CURIOUS
FOX
BOOKS

ABOUT THE AUTHOR

Wayne L. Wilson has written numerous biographical and historical books for children and young adults. He received a Master of Arts in education with a specialization in sociology and anthropology from UCLA. He is also a screenwriter and member of the Writer's Guild of America.

© 2024 by Curious Fox Books™, an imprint of Fox Chapel Publishing Company, Inc., 903 Square Street, Mount Joy, PA 17552.

Peaceful Protests: Voices for Peace is a revision of *I Protest: A History of Peaceful Protest: Voices for Peace*, published in 2018 by Purple Toad Publishing, Inc. Reproduction of its contents is strictly prohibited without written permission from the rights holder.

Paperback ISBN 979-8-89094-022-3
Hardcover ISBN 979-8-89094-023-0

Library of Congress Control Number: 2023947074

To learn more about the other great books from Fox Chapel Publishing, or to find a retailer near you, call toll-free 800-457-9112 or visit us at *www.FoxChapelPublishing.com*.

We are always looking for talented authors. To submit an idea, please send a brief inquiry to acquisitions@foxchapelpublishing.com.

Fox Chapel Publishing makes every effort to use environmentally friendly paper for printing.

Printed in Malaysia

CONTENTS

CHAPTER ONE
Early Antiwar Movements

*Peace is not merely a distant goal that we seek, but
a means by which we arrive at that goal. We must
pursue peaceful ends through peaceful means.*
—Martin Luther King Jr.[1]

For thousands of years, wars have been fought between villages,
kingdoms, and nations. We often read about wars or hear people
talk about them. But is any armed conflict a war? No. To be a war,
a conflict must be ongoing and claim more than 1,000 lives.[2] Not
everyone agrees that war is the answer to differences among
people. Protesters have risked their reputation, their freedom, and
their lives to speak out against war. In the end, though, peaceful
protests have often prevented or ended wars. This book covers a
few of these historic protests.

World War I Protests
Jane Addams was a dedicated peace activist. During World War I,
she started the Woman's Peace Party (WPP). In 1915, the WPP
held a major conference in Washington, D.C. Three thousand
women attended. They formed a Peace Platform that promoted

Jane Addams was founder of the Woman's Peace Party. Addams is pictured here (front row, second from left) in 1915 with the U.S. delegation to the International Committee of Women for a Permanent Peace at The Hague, Netherlands.

Jane Addams

"continuous mediation."[3] They wanted to use mediation, or peace talks, to resolve any arguments between the warring parties.

Later that year, Addams attended a peace conference at The Hague in the Netherlands. There, women from around the world created the Women's International League for Peace and Freedom (WILPF). They developed a plan for peace between the warring countries. Addams was chosen as its leader. She wrote hundreds of letters, organized peace conferences, and testified before the U.S. House of Representatives. Their plan was not adopted,

Jane Addams (behind the *P*) sails to the Netherlands with delegates from the International Committee of Women. The group would meet with leaders of 14 European countries, asking them to sign a peace pact.

and the United States entered the war in 1917.

Addams continued to fight for peace. Although she eventually lost much of her public support, she persisted. In 1931, she was awarded the Nobel Peace Prize, and her reputation was restored.[4]

Besides WILPF, another peace organization came out of the WPP: the American Civil Liberties Union (ACLU). These two groups continue to be active and effective in advocating for peace, freedom, justice, nonviolence, human rights, and equality.

Jane Addams speaks at Hull House in Chicago. She cofounded this settlement home with Ellen Gates Starr.

SANE

The National Committee for a Sane Nuclear Policy (SANE) was founded in 1957. Writers and activists Lenore Marshall, Norman Cousins, and Clarence Pickett created the organization to end the nuclear arms race. At the time, several nations, including the United States and the USSR, were testing nuclear weapons. SANE wanted the insanity to stop.

Hollywood stars helped spread the message, including Marlon Brando, Steve Allen, Henry Fonda, Marilyn Monroe, and Harry Belafonte. In 1960, SANE held a rally in Madison Square Garden, New York. It attracted 20,000 people and featured speakers such as former first lady Eleanor Roosevelt, Walter Reuther of the United Automobile Workers, and A. Philip Randolph of the Brotherhood of Sleeping Car Workers. Afterward, the speakers led 5,000 people on a march to the United Nations for a midnight prayer.[5]

Folk singer and activist Pete Seeger (center left) performs at the 1961 New York City Easter march, sponsored by SANE. About 3,500 people participated in this "Ban the Bomb" movement.

In 1961, SANE organized an eight-day, 109-mile march. It started at McGuire Air Force Base in New Jersey and ended in New York City at the United Nations Plaza. More than 25,000 people attended the "April Peace Mobilizations." Their aim was to convince President John F. Kennedy to stop testing nuclear weapons.[6]

SANE also organized protests against the Vietnam War, including marches in 1965 and 1966.

Other organizations and movements had similar goals. The Nuclear Freeze campaign worked to stop the use of nuclear weapons through marches and legislative action. In 1982, Nuclear Freeze organized a march in New York City that drew 750,000 protesters.

In 1987, SANE and Nuclear Freeze joined together. They changed their name to Peace Action in 1993. This grassroots organization became one of the largest peace groups in the United States. By 2023, it had around 100 chapters and 100,000 paying members.[7]

Women Strike For Peace

*I cannot bear the thought of this beautiful planet
spinning timelessly in space—without life.*
—Bertrand Russell, 1950 Nobel Prize–winning philosopher[8]

When Dagmar Wilson read Russell's statement, she felt inspired. But it also made her afraid. She had three daughters. What was this arms race doing to her children and other children's health?

She met with other concerned women to figure out how to stop this nuclear weapons race. The United States and the USSR were both testing nuclear weapons, each trying to develop more of them faster. Nuclear testing left radiation that harmed the environment and everything in it. The women were also upset about the "duck-and-cover" civil defense drills in schools. Every day, an alarm would sound, and students would have to "duck" under their desks and "cover" their heads. This was a psychological ploy to trick people into thinking a nuclear blast could be survived, while also brainwashing children to live in fear. Meanwhile, the government was pushing for a costly and scary fallout shelter program, which were designed to protect people in case of a nuclear war.

The group that Wilson gathered became Women Strike for Peace (WSP). Bella Abzug, already a respected activist, soon joined the group. The women made lists of people

Schools showed a *Duck and Cover* cartoon in which a turtle named Bert safely ducks into his shell when a monkey approaches with a burning stick of dynamite.

to call to join them. They handed out notices to announce a women's strike against the bomb. Their goal was a one-day nationwide strike that would draw attention to their cause.

Weeks later, the nation heard them.

On November 1, 1961, WSP brought together 50,000 women in 60 cities to march against nuclear weapons. Armed with the slogan, "An End to the Nuclear Arms Race, Not the Human Race," it was the largest national women's peace protest of the twentieth century.[9] More than 1,000 women picketed the White House. Delegations traveled to the USSR. They sent letters to First Lady Jacqueline Kennedy and Nina Petrovna Khrushchev, wife of Soviet leader Nikita Khrushchev. The letters asked these powerful women to join WSP and help end the arms race.

The great success of the one-day strike sparked an ongoing movement. Women organized, lobbied, demonstrated, and, as Dagmar Wilson stated: "[raised] a hue and cry against nuclear weapons."[10] In 1963, WSP helped to push the United States and the Soviet Union into signing a nuclear test-ban treaty.

The WSP continued to call for nuclear disarmament, and they were part of the broader peace movement against the Vietnam War. They also joined forces with Coretta Scott King and other leaders working for civil rights in America.

On November 1, 1963, Coretta Scott King (right) joined Dagmar Wilson (left) to march on the United Nations for disarmament.

BERTRAND RUSSELL

Bertrand Russell

Bertrand Russell was a mathematician, educator, peace activist, and author. He wrote over 70 books and thousands of essays. Their subjects ranged from serious topics to things that happen in everyday life. Russell strongly believed that ideas could change the world.

Russell was born in 1872 to a wealthy family in the United Kingdom. His mother and sister died when he was only two, and his father died just under two years later. He and his brother lived with his grandparents. Russell's grandfather served twice as the prime minister of Great Britain.

Russell studied at Cambridge University, and then worked as a professor, lecturer, and writer. He supported women's right to vote and took a strong antiwar stance. In 1918, he was jailed for opposing World War I. He was jailed again in 1961 for opposing nuclear weapons and the Vietnam War.

In 1950, Russell was awarded the Nobel Prize in Literature for promoting freedom of thought. In 1963, the Bertrand Russell Peace Foundation was established to support his work for "peace, human rights, and social justice."[11]

Bertrand Russell remained an outspoken peace activist until his death in 1970. He always believed peace was possible. Two days before he died, he issued a statement condemning Israel's bombing raids in the Middle East.

Vietnam War Protests

An eye for an eye only ends up making the whole world blind.
—*Mahatma Gandhi*[1]

By 1960, many U.S. college students were speaking out against the Vietnam War. Once a young man turned 18, he was required to register for the draft. Men who were enrolled in college were deferred from the draft. They would not have to serve until they left or finished college. Those who could not afford college were drafted in much higher numbers than those who could.

The voting age was 21. It angered students that they were considered too young to vote, but not too young to be sent into combat.[2] (The voting age was finally lowered to 18 when the 26th Amendment was passed on July 1, 1971.)

Young people wanted to have a say in the major decisions affecting their lives. They wanted to be able to vote on nuclear bomb testing, civil rights, and the war. To address these issues, they formed the group Students for a Democratic Society (SDS) in 1960. SDS was heavily influenced by the civil rights movement and the sit-ins organized by civil rights activists in Greensboro, North Carolina.[3]

Students for a Democratic Society hold a national council meeting in Bloomington, Indiana, in 1963.

On May 2, 1964, 1,000 students marched through New York City to the United Nations. Another 700 students marched through San Francisco. Smaller demonstrations were held in Boston, Madison (Wisconsin), and Seattle. The "May 2nd Movement" helped spread the word about the Vietnam War to thousands more students. Many considered this the first major student protest march.[4]

The Free Speech Movement

In the fall of 1964, University of California (UC) at Berkeley students returned to campus. Many of them had done civil rights work all summer. Students in the Mississippi Freedom Summer program helped register black people to vote. They wanted to continue their political activities at school.

The Free Speech Movement began at the University of California, Berkeley, in the fall of 1964.

Hundreds of demonstrators protested outside the president's office in Sproul Hall in Berkeley. The students demanded to be allowed to exercise their constitutional rights to free speech on campus.

University administrators stopped the students from using the campus for political speeches. Students felt that their rights to free speech and academic freedom were being violated, so they formed the Free Speech Movement (FSM). This organization was a combination of civil rights activists and antiwar crusaders. They started out protesting against the administration's ban on campus political activities. Then they organized debates, protests, sit-ins, and "teach-ins" on campuses across the country. At these teach-ins, students and teachers talked about the politics, current activity, and numbers of people injured and killed in the Vietnam War.[5]

The March on Washington

In 1965, President B. Lyndon Johnson escalated the war by sending an additional 175,000 combat troops into Vietnam.[6] The SDS responded. Its March on Washington to End the War in Vietnam was the largest peace protest of its

The March on Washington to End the War in Vietnam
was the largest peace march of its time.

time. It is estimated that 25,000 people met at the nation's capital on April 17, 1965. Most of them were college students.

March on Washington
official button

The all-day event began with demonstrators picketing outside the White House. Antiwar music and speeches were made at the base of the Washington Monument. Civil rights leader Bob Moses talked to the audience about how the peace and civil rights movements had come together with the common goal of getting the troops out of Vietnam.[7]

The media began posting graphic photographs of war casualties. One magazine showed children severely burned by U.S. napalm attacks in Vietnam. When he saw the magazine, Martin Luther King Jr. was horrified. He told a friend, "Nothing will ever taste good for me until I do everything I can to end that war."[8]

An emotional King told a church filled with 3,000 people that the war was an enemy of the poor and black soldiers. He explained that black people did not have equal rights in America. They were also being drafted in unfairly large numbers and sent thousands of miles away to fight for the rights of people in a foreign land. He wondered, how do you tell a young radical to go after their civil rights using nonviolent methods when the nation was using violence to achieve peace in Vietnam?[9]

Dr. Martin Luther King Jr. Marches Against the War

On March 25, 1967, Martin Luther King Jr. led a march of 5,000 antiwar demonstrators down State Street in Chicago. The marchers called for a cease-fire and for all troops to come home from Vietnam. A month later in New York City, King joined the Spring Mobilization Committee to End the War in

Martin Luther King Jr. leads an antiwar demonstration down State Street in Chicago in 1967.

Risking arrest and jail time, some people protested the Vietnam War by burning their draft cards.

Vietnam. He marched arm-in-arm with other leaders in this massive peace demonstration. Somewhere between 125,000 and 400,000 nonviolent protesters assembled in Central Park and marched across town to the United Nations for speeches and a rally.[10] Some protesters burned their draft cards. The protesters were hit with eggs and paint from those who disagreed with their antiwar views—but the protesters remained peaceful.

HIPPIES AND FLOWER POWER

In the 1960s, many young people became a part of the growing hippie movement. Hippies, or hipsters, did not trust the government, or what they called "the establishment." They expressed themselves by wearing long hair and colorful clothing, and by listening to rock 'n' roll music. They let people know that they would not be told how to look or how to act. "Peace and love" was their motto.

Hippies played a large role in the peaceful demonstrations against the war in Vietnam. One of their main slogans was "Flower Power!" This phrase came from poet and activist Allen Ginsberg, who suggested using peace as a "weapon." He urged protesters to carry peaceful "weapons" such as flowers, smiles, and songs.

On October 21, 1967, hippies armed with flowers gathered in an antiwar protest in Washington, D.C. Over 100,000 people showed up. During this demonstration, Bernie Boston, a news photographer, took a picture of an antiwar protester sticking carnations in the rifle barrels of soldiers guarding the Pentagon. It became one of the most famous pictures of that era. He called it *Flower Power*.[11]

High school student Jan Rose Kasmir confronts the American National Guard outside the Pentagon during the 1967 anti-Vietnam march.

Nonviolence is a power which can be wielded equally by all—children, young men and women, or grown-up people, provided they have a living faith in the God of Love and have therefore equal love for all mankind.[1]
—Mahatma Gandhi

In 1916, Jeannette Rankin became the first woman elected to Congress. During her term, Rankin introduced a bill that became the 19th Amendment to the Constitution. This amendment granted women the right to vote.

Rankin made many trips to India, where she studied the teachings of Mahatma Gandhi. They inspired her to devote the rest of her career to being an activist and pacifist. Rankin organized and led many antiwar marches in her lifetime. On January 15, 1968, at the age of 87, she led a women's march in Washington, D.C. They were protesting the Vietnam War. There hadn't been a women's march that large since the Woman Suffrage Parade of 1913.[2]

Four years after suffragist Jeannette Rankin became the first woman to serve in Congress, women won the right to vote. Rankin famously said: "I'm no lady; I'm a member of Congress."

A bronze statue of Jeannette Rankin stands in the U.S. Capitol's Statuary Hall.

Known as the Jeannette Rankin Brigade, 5,000 women met at D.C.'s Union Station. They marched silently, many dressed in black, to the steps of the Capitol Building. Rankin's banner read: "End the War in Vietnam and Social Crisis at Home!" Folk singer Judy Collins led marchers with songs such as "This Land Is Your Land" and "America."

The march was considered a success when Congress received the women's petition. However, Congress did not respond.

One thing that came out of the Brigade was the phrase "Sisterhood Is Powerful." It has been a hugely popular slogan for feminists. Today there is a statue of Jeannette Rankin in the Capitol's Statuary Hall. It is carved with the words, "I cannot vote for war."[3]

The Moratorium to End the War in Vietnam in 1969 became the largest political rally in the nation's history. Two million people joined the Peace Moratorium in October, and more than 500,000 protesters marched on Washington in November.

The Peace Moratorium

One of the most shocking events that happened in Vietnam was the My Lai Massacre. In March 1968, U.S. soldiers killed hundreds of unarmed civilians in the village of My Lai. There was a massive cover-up. When the public heard about it a year later, people were outraged.

They made their feelings known on October 15, 1969. Two million people across the country joined "The Peace Moratorium."[4] This demonstration put the Vietnam War in the world's spotlight. Approximately 250,000 demonstrators gathered outside the Capitol. Protesters heard speeches and expressed their anger and frustration over the war. Some demonstrators stayed through the night, singing and holding a candlelit vigil until more rallies started the next morning. Some supporters wore black armbands in tribute to the 45,000 Americans killed in the war.[5]

Moratorium March on Washington

Exactly one month later, on November 15, another demonstration was arranged. More than 500,000 people marched on Washington in an effort to put an end to the war.[6] It was the largest political rally in the country's history. It showed that the antiwar movement was made up of more than just militant youth. People from all walks of life got involved in the peace effort. Demonstrations took shape around the world, from San Francisco to as far away as London, England.

Some veterans returned to the United States no longer in favor of the war. They opposed U.S. policy in Vietnam and believed what they had done in the war was wrong. They organized resistance against the war. The soldiers formed groups such as Vietnam Veterans Against the War (VVAW). Soldiers and peace groups worked together organizing protests and printing underground newspapers. Coffeehouses in particular served as places for antiwar activities.

Veterans were shown little support on their return home. Some were even spat upon. Many of them suffered physically and mentally. Some were missing limbs, and some were sick from the toxins used in the war. Veterans found themselves jobless, and many sank into deep depressions. VVAW sought to bring healing to those who suffered from these and other effects of the war.

Many returning soldiers joined hands with other peace groups to organize major protests.

MUHAMMAD ALI: "JUST TAKE ME TO JAIL!"

Muhammad Ali, heavyweight boxing champion of the world, was in his prime when he received his draft card. As a Muslim, he believed in peace. He declared he was a conscientious objector and refused to serve. He said: "Man, I ain't got no quarrel with them Viet Cong. . . . they never lynched me, they didn't put no dogs on me, they didn't rob me of my nationality. . . . Shoot them for what? . . . . Just take me to jail!"[7]

In 1967, Ali was arrested and convicted of draft dodging. His boxing license was suspended and his title was stripped. Many Americans hated him.

Ali was given many chances to change his mind and join the military. He would not have to fight, but could perform in boxing exhibitions. He still refused. Instead, Ali continued his fight in the courts. He spoke on college campuses about race relations and the Vietnam War.

In 1971, the Supreme Court finally overturned Ali's conviction, and his boxing license was reinstated. Ali's war stance came at a great personal cost. The champ was stripped of his best fighting years, and he lost millions of dollars. While many people considered him a coward for not putting his life on the line, others called him a hero for standing up for his beliefs.

Muhammad Ali is escorted from the armed forces examining station in Houston after refusing to participate in the war.

CHAPTER FOUR
The Struggle for Peace

If America's soul becomes totally poisoned, part of the autopsy must read "Vietnam."
—Martin Luther King Jr.[1]

In 1971, more than 200,000 antiwar protesters, including Vietnam veterans, demonstrated in front of the Capitol Building in Washington, D.C. The three-day demonstration was called the "May Day Protest," and not just because it happened in May. The word "mayday" is used as an international distress signal or call for help. The war had escalated, and thousands of people were dying. Demonstrators viewed this protest as a plea for help in saving soldiers' lives.

The feeling was that no one in President Richard Nixon's administration was listening to them. The protesters decided that in order to be heard, they would try to shut down the government for at least a day. Calling themselves the May Day Tribe, the protesters promised: "If the government will not stop the war, we will stop the government!"[2]

As the war escalated, casualties increased. People from all economic levels, walks of life, and even other countries joined the antiwar movement. It became much harder for the U.S. government to ignore the constant cries for peace.

Before the demonstration began, the protesters received maps to all the key locations and a description of the bridges and traffic circles. Armed with a plan, they went to the targeted areas. They blocked roads with cars, trashcans, and self-made barricades. Some protesters lay down in the streets to keep government employees from getting to work.

Thousands of protesters camped out at West Potomac Park. They listened to rock music, danced, and did what they could to interfere with the daily activities in the area. President Nixon called in the military and National Guard to aid the thousands of police already in place. They were told to arrest any demonstrator they spotted.

The police mowed through the crowd. They used pepper spray and billy clubs to scatter the protesters. They chased protesters through the streets. One protester recalled, "Any time you stood still you'd be arrested, so you had to keep moving."[3]

More than 200,000 protesters demanded an end to the Vietnam War at the nation's capital in May 1971.

Even under arrest, May Day protesters made a stand for peace.

Over 7,000 protesters were arrested on May 3. Another 6,000 were arrested over the next couple of days. It was the largest number of arrests for a single event in U.S. history. There weren't enough city jails for all of them. The police jammed twenty people into two-person cells. Another 1,500 demonstrators were placed in the jail's recreational yard. The rest of them were held on the Washington Commanders football field, which was fenced in for the occasion. Many people felt sorry for the protesters. They threw food, blankets, and notes of encouragement over the fence to them.[4]

The May Day protests did not accomplish the mission of shutting down the U.S. government. But the protesters did receive a lot of sympathy. More people became more aware of the situation in Vietnam. They joined in criticizing the president for how he was handling the war.

The Lexington Green Protest

The Revolutionary War started with the Battles of Lexington and Concord on April 19, 1775. This bloody conflict between Massachusetts farmers and British soldiers occurred on the now historic Lexington Green. On May 30, 1971, Vietnam Veterans Against the War, with the support of

Angry vets march for jobs. Veterans held many protests across the country.

the townspeople, conducted a three-day march from Concord to Boston. More than 450 nonviolent protesters occupied Lexington Green.

The protesters refused to leave the grounds. No one was allowed to sleep or camp in that area after 10:00 p.m., but the protesters stayed. At 3:00 a.m. on Sunday, they were rounded up and arrested.[5]

VVAW had chosen Lexington Green because they identified with the minutemen of the Revolutionary War who were prepared to go to battle at a minute's notice. The locals of New England were proud of their heritage. When the patriots broke the "king's laws," it was always for the higher good.

Unlike during the May Day arrests, many of the police officers were courteous. Some even apologized for throwing people in jail. The protesters were tried, convicted, and fined five dollars. Moving on, they continued their march to Boston. Their demonstration increased public interest in bringing about peace and an end to the Vietnam War.

The United States began pulling troops out of Vietnam in 1973. The war there ended two years later.

People hoped that this war would be the last. Unfortunately, more would follow.

PROTEST AND MUSIC

John Lennon, musician and former member of The Beatles, set the stage for one of the most memorable peace demonstrations of all time. He and his wife, artist Yoko Ono, were very active in the protest against the Vietnam War. On March 25, 1969, John and Yoko invited the international media to join them in their hotel suite for a week of "Bed-Ins for Peace." They wore pajamas, and their entire suite was decorated with flowers. During the bed-in, Lennon wrote and recorded the antiwar song "Give Peace a Chance."[6]

Other musicians used their talents to protest the Vietnam War. Bob Dylan wrote "The Times They Are A-Changin" and "Blowin' in the Wind." Folk singer Joan Baez led protest marches with Pete Seeger's song "We Shall Overcome." Creedence Clearwater Revival wrote about the unfair draft rules in "Fortunate Son." Crosby, Stills, Nash & Young's "Ohio" described the slaying of four college students who were protesting the war at Ohio's Kent State University.[7]

John and Yoko at the Bed-In.

The Woodstock music festival in August 1969 was one of the world's greatest music events and became associated with the movement because of the many antiwar protesters who attended. It spread the music of peace to an audience of nearly half a million people. On the last day, concertgoers were treated to Jimi Hendrix performing a heartfelt version of "The Star-Spangled Banner." The decade of the sixties closed with Edwin Starr's antiwar anthem, with the lyrics, "WAR! What is it good for? Absolutely nothing!"[8]

Wars are poor chisels for carving out peaceful tomorrows.
–Martin Luther King Jr.[1]

In January 2003, rallies against a possible war in Iraq were held in Washington, D.C. and San Francisco. Civil rights activist Jesse Jackson addressed a peace rally of thousands of people on the National Mall in Washington. He preached, "Let's choose minds over missiles and negotiation over confrontation."[2]

On February 15, 2003, the cries, "The World Says No to War" and "No Blood for Oil" were heard in many languages and from millions of people. Protesters all over the world marched through the streets of nearly 800 large cities and tiny villages in places like Australia, New Zealand, Asia, Europe, Africa, Latin America, and the United States. The *Guinness World Records 2004* book notes that between 12 and 14 million people demonstrated that day.[3] It was viewed as the largest protest in the history of the world. Despite the protests, the George W. Bush administration decided to go to war in Iraq.[4]

British antiwar protesters march outside army headquarters in Northwood, Middlesex, in 2003, as part of "The World Says No to War" movement.

Family and friends of the Sheehan family hold a photo of U.S. Army Specialist Casey Sheehan, who was killed during the Iraq War.

The "Camp Casey" Protests

Cindy Sheehan is the mother of a 19-year-old soldier who died in the Iraq War. In the summer of 2005, she started a movement. While President Bush was on vacation, she camped outside his ranch in Crawford, Texas. She wanted to ask the president "for what noble cause" her son, Casey, had died.

Sheehan's vigil made front-page news across the United States. Thousands of people people joined her at "Camp Casey," named in honor of her son. They held a vigil for one month near the ranch, sharing food and stories of grief caused by the war.[5]

Cindy Sheehan never met with the president, but her mission didn't end there. Many groups took on her cause. Military organizations, such as the Iraq

Veterans Against the War, Veterans for Peace, Military Families Speak Out, and Gold Star Families for Peace, organized bus tours called "Bring Them Home Now." These groups joined the larger peace movement and participated in speaking events, memorials, media interviews, town halls, prayer vigils, marches, and meetings with politicians. Cindy Sheehan participated in many of these affairs.

Other protests continued as well. On March 17, 2007, St. Patrick's Day, thousands of antiwar demonstrators marched from the Vietnam War Memorial across the Potomac River to the Pentagon. They carried yellow-and-black signs, reading, "U.S. Out of Iraq Now!" Speakers called for President Bush and his administration to be impeached. An antiwar rally was also held in Los Angeles,

Students for a Democratic Society members unite during an antiwar demonstration in Washington, D.C., in March 2007.

drawing 5,000 to 6,000 protesters. Many demonstrators carried signs in Spanish and displayed fake coffins covered with the American flag.[6]

Two years later, protesters again marched on the Pentagon. Iraq and Afghanistan War veterans and members of ANSWER (the Act Now to Stop War and End Racism) Coalition led the demonstration. The crowd included members of Arab and Muslim communities. They marched into downtown Crystal City, Virginia, where the leading military suppliers Boeing, Lockheed Martin, and General Dynamics were headquartered. The protesters carried signs that read, "Merchants of Death."[7]

On March 17, 2007, the 40th anniversary of the anti-Vietnam War March on the Pentagon, thousands marched again, demanding the U.S. immediately get out of Iraq.

Veterans marched the downtown streets of hot, humid Chicago on May 20, 2012, against the wars in Afghanistan and Iraq.

Veterans March for Justice

The wars in Iraq and Afghanistan continued. On Sunday, May 20, 2012, thousands of protesters in Chicago marched beside Iraq and Afghanistan war veterans. The demonstration was called the Veterans March for Justice and Reconciliation. The veterans wanted to return their service medals to NATO's generals. Chicago police officers protected the generals. They shut down the section around McCormick Place where the conference was being held.

A stage was quickly set up near the conference site. During the emotional speeches, one veteran said, "These medals once made me feel good . . . but I came back to reality. I don't like these anymore." Another veteran said: "My unit spearheaded the attack on most major cities during the war, and I saw or

participated in much of the initial destruction. I was in a heavy missile artillery unit, and we were responsible for over 5,000 indiscriminate casualties."[8] At the end of the speeches, the veterans threw their medals at the convention center as the crowd cheered.

U.S. involvement in Middle East wars continued. In 2015 in Los Angeles and Washington, D.C., protesters rallied against U.S. involvement in Iraq, Syria, Afghanistan, and Palestine.

When Donald J. Trump became U.S. president in 2017, he immediately placed travel bans against Muslims from certain Middle Eastern countries.

Protesters against the Muslim ban marched in many cities and occupied airports across the country.

He claimed it was an effort to curb terrorism in the United States. Thousands of people marched in protest, including the Minnesota Anti-War Committee. Members of this group marched on the Minneapolis Federal Building, carrying banners that read: "No Attacks on Muslims!"; "No to War and Racism!"; and "No Racist Walls or Wars!"

Peaceful demonstrations have often proven to be the most effective weapon in preventing and stopping wars. The strategy continues to be vital. In an age of deadly accurate technology and highly advanced weapons, the need for people to speak out against war has never been more important.

WOMEN OF LIBERIA MASS ACTION FOR PEACE

Leymah Gbowee

In 2002, social worker Leymah Gbowee recruited hundreds of Christian women to protest the civil war that had been going on for 15 years in Liberia. More than 200,000 people had died in the war.

She remarked: "In the past we were silent. . . . War taught us that the future lies in saying NO to violence and YES to peace."[9] Muslim women joined with Christian women. They organized peace vigils in churches and mosques.

The women held their first major protest in 2003. Their shirts and banners proclaimed: "The women of Liberia want peace now!"[10] Over 2,500 women gathered on the fish market lawn each day. They held sit-ins, danced, and sang for peace. The fish market was very close to the presidential palace. President Charles Taylor's motorcade passed the women every day.

On April 11, 1,000 women marched on the Municipal Office in Monrovia (the capital).[11] The president sent armed men to beat the women, but they persisted. The president offered them $5,000 to end their protest, but the women refused. They said, "Money cannot buy peace."[12]

President Taylor and the rebels finally agreed to peace talks to be held in Ghana. The women sat outside the presidential palace, linking arms. They did not let anyone leave the building until the peace talks were settled. When the guards tried to arrest them, Gbowee threatened to remove her clothes. (This would have shamed the men, according to their traditions.) The guards backed away and left them alone. After a while, the Ghanaian president allowed the women to come inside and join the discussions.

On August 11, Taylor resigned as president of Liberia and the terms for peace were announced. In 2005, the Liberian people elected their first female president—Ellen Johnson Sirleaf. Gbowee and Sirleaf shared the Nobel Peace Prize in 2011.

Leymah Gbowee (left) and Ellen Johnson Sirleaf (right) receive the 2011 Nobel Peace Prize "for their nonviolent struggle for the safety of women and for women's rights."[13]

TIMELINE

1915	A group of 68 pacifists founds the United States Fellowship of Reconciliation. Jane Addams starts the Woman's Peace Party.
1917	The American Union Against Militarism is formed in response to World War I.
1920	After World War I, the League of Nations is formed. The United States does not join.
1921	The Woman's Peace Union organizes to promote peace and outlaw war.
1938	The Keep America Out of War Congress is founded.
1940	America First Committee is formed. It is the largest antiwar organization in American history.
1948	The Progressive Party peace movement begins.
1959	The Workers World Party is formed.
1960	Students for a Democratic Society (SDS) is founded.
1961	Women Strike for Peace march against nuclear weapons.
1964	The Free Speech Movement arises on the UC Berkeley campus.
1965	President Lyndon B. Johnson increases U.S. military forces in Vietnam and starts bombing North Vietnam. SDS organizes its first Vietnam War teach-in at the University of Michigan. Draft card burning takes place at Berkeley. Vietnam Day Committee organizes the largest Vietnam teach-in with 30,000 people. The Vietnam War protests draw over 100,000 people in cities across the U.S. On November 27, over 35,000 antiwar protesters march on the White House.
1966	Antiwar demonstrations take place in many cities across the United States and around the world. Ten thousand people picket the White House. Students take over the administration building at the University of Chicago to protest the draft.
1967	An antiwar rally in New York City draws 400,000 people. Vietnam Veterans Against the War (VVAW) is formed. Dr. Martin Luther King Jr. delivers a monumental antiwar speech called "Beyond Vietnam" and leads a march. Stop the Draft Week organizers lead 3,000 marchers to California's Oakland Army Induction Center, where they sit outside. Draftees are forced to climb over them to get inside the building.
1968	Antiwar protesters march in several U.S. cities, including 87,000 in Central Park, New York. Massive protests are staged at the Democratic National Convention.
1969	Between 300,000 and 500,000 people gather at Woodstock for a three-day festival to promote peace and music. More than 250,000 march in Washington, D.C. for peace. John Lennon and Yoko Ono hold a Bed-In for Peace. *Tinker v. Des Moines Independent Community School District* U.S. Supreme Court decision defines the First Amendment rights of students in public schools.
1971	Approximately 500,000 protesters rally at the U.S. Capitol, petitioning for an end to the war. In San Francisco, 200,000 antiwar demonstrators rally. The U.S. Supreme Court unanimously overturns Muhammad Ali's conviction for draft resistance. VVAW sponsors The Winter Soldier Investigation to gather stories from soldiers regarding war crimes in Vietnam.

1973	U.S. military involvement in Vietnam ends with a ceasefire and withdrawal.
1975	The North Vietnamese take Saigon (now Ho Chi Minh City). The Vietnam War ends.
1991	In downtown Seattle, Washington, 2,500 antiwar protesters march against the Gulf War in the Middle East.
1995	Student Peace Action Network forms to recruit young activists.
2002	Outside the United Nations in New York, over 1,000 people protest. They chant, "No Blood For Oil" while President George W. Bush speaks. One thousand people attend an antiwar protest in Chicago. They listen to speeches by Jesse Jackson and Senator Barack Obama. Tens of thousands of protesters in Washington, D.C. (100,000) and San Francisco (50,000) demonstrate against the war.
2003	Act Now to Stop War and End Racism (ANSWER) begins a massive U.S. antiwar movement regarding the U.S. invasion of Iraq. Millions worldwide protest the war with Iraq.
2004	Iraq war protesters demonstrate at the Women's Memorial at Arlington National Cemetery for the National Memorial Procession.
2005	Cindy Sheehan, mother of slain soldier Casey Sheehan, sets up a protest camp outside President Bush's ranch in Crawford, Texas. Thousands join her vigil.
2006	On the third anniversary of the invasion of Iraq, major protests are held worldwide.
2007	Veterans for Peace and ANSWER organize 100,000 people to march from the White House to the Capitol to protest the war.
2009	Thousands of protesters march from the National Mall in Washington, D.C., to the grounds of the Pentagon and then to Crystal City. They carry mock coffins representing the victims of U.S. conflicts.
2012	Thousands of protesters march with Iraq and Afghanistan war veterans in Chicago. The veterans try to return their service medals to NATO's generals.
2015	In Los Angeles and Washington, D.C., protesters rally against U.S. involvement in Iraq, Syria, Afghanistan, and Palestine.
2017	The Minnesota Anti-War Committee marches against President Donald J. Trump's Muslim ban and U.S. involvement in wars overseas.
2022	Demonstrations are held in many major U.S. cities to protest Russia's invasion of Ukraine. There are also protests within Russia and hundreds are arrested and face criminal prosecution.

CHAPTER NOTES

Chapter 1: Early Antiwar Movements

1. "King Quotes on War and Peace," Stanford: The Martin Luther King Research and Education Institute. https://kinginstitute.stanford.edu/liberation-curriculum/classroom-resources/king-quotes-war-and-peace

2. Chris Hedges, "What Every Person Should Know About War," *The New York Times*, July 6, 2003. https://www.nytimes.com/2003/07/06/books/chapters/what-every-person-should-know-about-war.html

3. "Jane Addams," Theodore Roosevelt Inaugural Site (National Park Service). https://www.nps.gov/thri/jane-addams.htm

4. Amy Swerdlow, *Women Strike For Peace: Traditional Motherhood and Radical Politics in the 1960s,* (Chicago: The University of Chicago Press, 1993), p. 45.

5. "Peace Action Timeline," *Peace Action*, https://www.peaceaction.org/who-we-are/our-mission/timeline/

6. "History," Peace Action, https://www.peaceaction.org/who-we-are/our-mission/history/

7. Ibid.

8. "Women's Strike For Peace." *Activists With Attitude: Thoughts on Courage and Creativity.* http://activistswithattitude.com/womens-strike-for-peace/

9. Kathy Crandall Robinson, "Women Strike For..." *The Huffington Post*, August 29, 2016. https://www.huffingtonpost.com/entry/women-strike-for_us_57c317bde4b00c54015e5928

10. Woo, Elaine. "Dagmar Wilson Dies at 94; Organizer of Women's Disarmament Protesters." *Los Angeles Times,* January 30, 2011. https://www.latimes.com/local/obituaries/la-xpm-2011-jan-30-la-me-dagmar-wilson-20110130-story.html

11. "Origins," Bertrand Russell Peace Foundation. http://www.russfound.org/about/about.htm

Chapter 2: Vietnam War Protests

1. Moving Words: "Mahatma Gandhi," BBC, https://www.bbc.co.uk/worldservice/learningenglish/movingwords/quotefeature/gandhi.shtml

2. Paul A. Bishop, "Vietnam Era Anti-War Activism." *American Anti-War Activism and Peace Movements.*

3. Sandra Gurvis, *Where Have All the Flower Children Gone?* (Jackson: University Press of Mississippi, 2006), pp. 4–5.

4. "What Is the May 2nd Movement?" Sixties Project. http://www2.iath.virginia.edu/sixties/HTML_docs/Resources/Primary/Manifestos/PL_M2d_manifesto.html

5. Gurvis, pp. 5–6.

6. Debbie Levy, *The Vietnam War: Chronicle of America's Wars* (Minneapolis: Lerner Publications, 2004), p. 27.

7. *Resistance and Revolution: The Anti-Vietnam War Movement at the University of Michigan, 1965–1972.* "The March on Washington." http://michiganintheworld.history.lsa.umich.edu/antivietnamwar/exhibits/show/exhibit/the_teach_ins/national_teach_in_1965

8. Matt Pearce, "Martin Luther King Jr. Fought for More than Civil Rights. This Was the Protest Less Remembered." *The Los Angeles* Times, January 16, 2017. https://www.latimes.com/nation/la-na-martin-luther-king-vietnam-20170113-story.html

9. Ibid.

10. "From Harlem to Hanoi: Dr. King and the Vietnam War." MCNY Blog: New York Stories. https://blog.mcny.org/2016/02/16/from-harlem-to-hanoi-dr-king-and-the-vietnam-war/

11. Adam Bernstein, "Bernie Boston, 74: Took Iconic 1967 Photograph." *Washington Post*, https://www.washingtonpost.com/wp-dyn/content/article/2008/01/23/AR2008012303713.html

Chapter 3: Joining the Antiwar Movement

1. Mazhar Kibriya, *Gandhi and Indian Freedom Struggle* (New Delhi; APH Publishing Corporation, 1999), p. 26.

2. Kelsey Matthews, "The Jeannette Rankin Brigade." *Boundary Stones*, August 24, 2016. https://boundarystones.weta.org/2016/08/24/jeannette-rankin-brigade

3. Ibid.

4. "1969: Millions March in U.S. Vietnam Moratorium," BBC, *On this Day, October 15,* http://news.bbc.co.uk/onthisday/hi/dates/stories/october/15/newsid_2533000/2533131.stm

5. "Moratorium Against the Vietnam War, November 15, 1969," *TIME*, https://content.time.com/time/specials/packages/article/0,28804,2080036_2080037_2080024,00.html
6. Ibid.
7. Krishnadev Calamur, "Muhammad Ali and Vietnam." *The Atlantic*, June 2016. https://www.theatlantic.com/news/archive/2016/06/muhammad-ali-vietnam/485717/

Chapter 4: The Struggle for Peace

1. Matt Pearce, "Martin Luther King Jr. Fought for More than Civil Rights. This Was the Protest Less Remembered." *The Los Angeles Times*, January 16, 2017. https://www.latimes.com/nation/la-na-martin-luther-king-vietnam-20170113-story.html
2. Global Nonviolent Action Database, "Washington, D.C. Protests Against the War in Vietnam (Mayday), 1971." https://nvdatabase.swarthmore.edu/content/washington-dc-protests-against-war-vietnam-mayday-1971
3. "Mayday 1971: Most Arrests in US History" *RT News.* https://www.rt.com/usa/mayday-usa-protesting-history/
4. Global Nonviolent Action Database.
5. "Vietnam Veterans Arrested on Lexington Green," *Mass Moments,* 2017. https://www.massmoments.org/moment-details/vietnam-veterans-arrested-on-lexington-green.html
6. Dave Lifton, "The Story of John Lennon and Yoko Ono's Bed-in for Peace," Classic Rock, March 5, 2016. https://ultimateclassicrock.com/john-lennon-yoko-ono-bed-in/
7. Kerry Candaele, "The Sixties and Protest Music," The Gilder Lehrman Institute of American History, https://www.gilderlehrman.org/history-resources/essays/sixties-and-protest-music
8. Alexander E. Hopkins, "Protest and Rock n' Roll During the Vietnam War," *Inquiries Journal*, http://www.inquiriesjournal.com/articles/713/protest-and-rock-n-roll-during-the-vietnam-war

Chapter 5: Protesting Wars in the Middle East

1. Martin Luther King, Jr., "The Casualties of the War in Vietnam." http://www.aavw.org/special_features/speeches_speech_king02.html
2. "Anti-war Demonstrators Rally Around the World," CNN, January 18, 2005. http://www.cnn.com/2003/US/01/18/sproject.irq.us.protests/
3. Phyllis Bennis, "February 15, 2003. The Day the World Said No to War." Institute for Policy Studies, https://www.ips-dc.org/february_15_2003_the_day_the_world_said_no_to_war/
4. Ishaan Tharoor, "Viewpoint: Why Was the Biggest Protest in World History Ignored?" *TIME*, February 15, 2013. https://world.time.com/2013/02/15/viewpoint-why-was-the-biggest-protest-in-world-history-ignored/
5. Lisa Leitz, *Fighting for Peace: Veterans and Military Families in the Anti-Iraq War Movement.* (Minneapolis: University of Minnesota Press, 2014), pp. 2–3.
6. Caren Bohan, "Thousands March to Protest Iraq War," *Reuters.* https://www.reuters.com/article/us-iraq-usa-protest-idUSN1725671220070317
7. "March 21, 2009," ANSWER (Act Now to Stop War & End Racism Coalition), https://www.answercoalition.org/march_21_2009
8. Allison Kilkenny, "Thousands March with Veterans for Peace at Chicago NATO Summit; Police Respond With Brute Force." *Truthout*, May 21, 2012. https://truthout.org/articles/thousands-march-with-veterans-for-peace-police-respond-with-brute-force/
9. Amanda Molinaro, "Women's Peace Movement of Liberia." *Peacemaker Heroes.* https://myhero.com/womens_peace_movement_liberia_08
10. "Liberian Women Act to End Civil War, 2003," Global Nonviolent Action Database, https://nvdatabase.swarthmore.edu/content/liberian-women-act-end-civil-war-2003
11. Ibid.
12. Molinaro.
13. Nobelprize.org. "Ellen Johnson Sirleaf—Facts." https://www.nobelprize.org/nobel_prizes/peace/laureates/2011/johnson_sirleaf-facts.html

FURTHER READING

Works Consulted

Gurvis, Sandra. *Where Have All the Flower Children Gone?* Jackson: University Press of Mississippi, 2006.

Kibriya, Mazhar. *Gandhi and Indian Freedom Struggle.* New Delhi: APH Publishing Corporation, 1999.

Kurlansky, Mark. *Nonviolence: Twenty-Five Lessons from the History of a Dangerous Idea.* New York: Modern Library, 2006.

Leitz, Lisa. *Fighting for Peace: Veterans and Military Families in the Anti-Iraq War Movement.* Minneapolis: University of Minnesota Press. 2014.

Robbins, Mary Susannah (Ed.). *Against the Vietnam War: Writings by Activists.* New York: Syracuse University Press, 1999.

Swerdlow, Amy, *Women Strike for Peace: Traditional Motherhood and Radical Politics in the 1960s.* Chicago: The University of Chicago Press, 1993.

Books for Young Readers

Cohen, Ronald D.; Will Kaufman. *Singing for Peace: Antiwar Songs in American History.* New York: Routledge—Taylor & Francis Group, 2015.

Cummings, Judy Dodge. *Rebels & Revolutions: Real Tales of Radical Change in America.* White River Junction, VT: Nomad Press, 2017.

Internet Reading

The Antiwar Movement.
https://www.ushistory.org/us/55d.asp

Candaele. Kerry. "The Sixties and Protest Music." History Now.
https://www.gilderlehrman.org/history-resources/essays/sixties-and-protest-music

Cassandra Gill, "11 Facts About the Modern Peace Movement." OUPblog (Oxford University Press), August 28, 2016.
https://blog.oup.com/2016/08/11-facts-modern-peace-movement/

History: Vietnam War Protests.
https://www.history.com/topics/vietnam-war/vietnam-war-protests

War Fever and Antiwar Protests. Digital History.
https://www.digitalhistory.uh.edu/disp_textbook.cfm?smtID=2&psid=3266

bayonet (BAY-uh-net)—A long knife that attaches to the end of a rifle.

coalition (koh-uh-LIH-shun)—A group of people or nations who have joined together for a common goal.

conscientious objector (kon-shee-EN-shus ob-JEK-ter)—Someone who will not serve in the military because of his or her moral or religious beliefs.

crisis (KRY-sis)—A dangerous situation or emergency.

escalation (es-kah-LAY-shun)—A rapid increase.

fallout (FALL-out)—A bad effect or result of something.

indiscriminate (in-dis-KRIH-mih-nit)—Done without caring about the harm an action could cause.

insurgent (in-SUR-jent)—A person who fights against the government or its laws. A rebel.

mobilization (moh-bul-ih-ZAY-shun)—Large groups of people working together for a certain action or event.

moratorium (mor-ah-TOR-ee-um)—The delay or stopping of a certain activity.

motto (MAH-toh)—A sentence, phrase, or word expressing the thoughts or purpose of a person or group.

napalm (NAY-palm)—A thick jelly that contains gasoline and is used in firebombs and flamethrowers. It can burn large areas at once.

NATO (NAY-toh)—Short for the North Atlantic Treaty Organization, this group of countries agrees to protect each other in times of war.

pacifist (PAS-ih-fist)—Someone who believes violence or war is wrong. He or she may refuse to fight or support a war because of that belief.

Pentagon (PEN-tih-gon)—The headquarters of the U.S. Department of Defense.

persist (per-SIST)—To continue to do something no matter how hard it is or how many people may tell you to stop.

petition (peh-TIH-shun)—A written document people sign that shows they want a person or organization to do or change something.

proliferation (proh-lih-fer-AY-shun)—A rapid increase in number or amount.

radiation (ray-dee-AY-shun)—The release of energy from a substance. The radiation of certain substances can be deadly.

radical (RAH-dih-kul)—A person who has social or political views that are not shared by most others.

rebellious (ree-BEL-yus)—Being in a state of refusing to obey rules or authority or to accept normal standards of behavior.

reformer (ree-FOR-mer)—A person who works to improve society or government.

resolution (reh-zuh-LOO-shun)—A formal statement of action adopted by a group.

suffrage (SUH-fridj)—The right to vote.

USSR (Union of Soviet Socialist Republics)—Also known as the Soviet Union, a country that was made up of 15 former countries in Europe and Asia. These countries became independent again when the USSR dissolved in 1991.

vigil (VIH-jul)—An event or period of time when a person or group stays in a place and quietly waits and prays.

PHOTO CREDITS: Cover—Igor Stevanovic, ZUMA Press; p. 8—Paul Greenberg; p. 13—C Clark Kissinger; p. 22—Aoc.gov; p.35—WMWC; p. 36—Vic Reinhart; p. 38—Masha George; p. 40—Fronteiras do Pensamento; p. 41—Utenriksdepartement et UD. All other photos—Public Domain. Every measure has been taken to find all copyright holders of material used in this book. In the event any mistakes or omissions have happened within, attempts to correct them will be made in future editions of the book.